SPALDING FLOWE

THE GOLDEN YEARS

Lincolnshire
free press

SPALDING
Guardian

at heart ♡ publications

T. LAW & SONS family butcher
FRESH MEAT
COOKED MEATS
Cardfair
WELCOME TO
2

Contents

First published in 2007 by:
At Heart Ltd, 32 Stamford Street, Altrincham,
Cheshire, WA14 1EY.
in conjunction with

Spalding Guardian & Lincolnshire Free Press
Priory House, The Crescent, Spalding, PE11 1AB

©2007 Spalding Guardian & Lincolnshire Free Press

ISBN : 978-1-84547-159-0

Printed by Bell & Bain Ltd, Scotland.

The Glory Days

By Doug Braybrooks

Christine Hanson suggested that I ought to write a book about Spalding Flower Parade when I was at her shop Bookmark, Spalding, for the launch of Rex Sly's book about the Fens, *From Punt to Plough*.

As the 50th Spalding Flower Parade approached it was apparent that there was no record of how or why it started.

There were also misconceptions regarding organisation and funding that I felt needed rectifying.

I thought that having been involved with organising the parade for 30 years or so I was as well placed as anybody to have a go at it.

So with the encouragement of Christine, my wife Wendy and others, I researched the beginnings of the parade and the bulb industry.

Nick Woodhead, editor of the *Lincolnshire Free Press* and *Spalding Guardian*, agreed to help bring the book to publication and the newspapers' archive was a valuable source of information.

With the founders of the industry, and the parade, now getting thin on the ground, I have tried to ensure accuracy by relying heavily on the official National Farmers' Union and Flower Parade minutes.

I have also used my own recollections and those of the people most directly concerned with putting on the show.

I have spent many hours with some of them, stirring up happy memories and recalling, in the words of Bruce Springsteen, the "Glory Days".

I have tried to include as many people as possible who have worked on, sponsored or helped with the parade, but with so many clubs, companies and individuals involved, it is almost inevitable that I will have missed some. To these people I apologise.

I hope that I have conveyed the imagination, commitment and enthusiasm of the people of Spalding and surrounding area who created and continue this world famous spectacle.

ACKNOWLEDGEMENTS

My thanks to:

Chris Hanson, Rex Sly, Stuart Gibbard and Petronella Keeling for their support and encouragement.

Lord Taylor CBE, David Norton, Rosemary Pilgrim and all at Springfields Horticultural Society and Steve Barber and staff at the National Farmers' Union for help and access to minutes and archive.

Nick Woodhead for access to *The Lincolnshire Free Press* and *Spalding Guardian* archive.

Barry Drew and Spalding Flower Parade and Carnival Trust, particularly Adrian Jansen, for his help in bringing me up to date.

Past chairmen Francis Hanson MBE, Dick Hill, Rob Teeuw, Roger Taylor, Brian Drury and George Slinger.

Peter Atkinson OBE, Nancy Mayfield, Chris Longstaff, Tom Maxey, Sheila Robson MBE, Peter Ruysen, Adrian van Egmond, Clive Gotobed, John Honnor, Dave Frankish, Rodney Flowers, Mick Flowers, Lawrence Wakefield, Karen Gerrard, Bruce and Caroline Goodwin, Vera Hart, Barbara Moore, Pip Lowther, Barbara Drury, Clayton Banks, Jim Horberry, Jim Welch, Keith Woods and Anthony Howling for their memories, facts and figures or photos.

Reg Dobbs OBE for sharing with me his vast knowledge of the bulb industry.

Geoff Dodd and Gordon Scott for hours spent reminiscing.

Many of the photographs, particularly those in the Springfields archive, could not be attributed to individual photographers, but would have included Bryan Simpson (Spring Photographic), Les Prudden, Brian Benson Art Services and Tim Wilson (*Lincolnshire Free Press* and *Spalding Guardian*).

Finally, I must thank my wife Wendy for her support and patience when I hogged her computer and buried her dining table under photos, minutes and old programmes.

Creation of a Spectacle

For centuries the Fens around the Wash have provided a bountiful harvest. The first settlements were on silt islands among the meres and creeks. The islands would provide rich grazing and land for cultivation and the meres and creeks would provide the fish, wildfowl, reeds and salt.

The Romans made improvements to the Fens. So, too, the Saxons who built banks to contain the rivers and hold back the sea. Many of today's roads still follow the course of those embankments.

In the 17th Century, wealthy landowners, known as adventurers, brought over Dutch engineers such as Vermuiden and Vernatti (after whom the Vernatts Drain is named), to push ahead with the drainage of the inland meres. Thousands of miles of drains and dykes were cut, by hand, and hundreds of brick bridges were built to carry the roads over them.

Not all were happy - the work was resisted, sometimes violently, by the Fen Slodgers, who had made their livings by wildfowling and fishing.

But they were unable to stop progress and soon the Fens were dry all year round, except for a few washes such as Cowbit, Crowland, Whittlesey and Welney, which still flooded in winter.

The newly-drained land proved to be as fertile as any in the world. Indeed, it was said that if you stuck a walking stick in the ground it would grow.

Spalding itself grew, with wealth brought by the wool trade, into a large and prosperous port with imposing houses along the High Street. New crops like potatoes and sugar beet were introduced with great success and a multitude of market gardens flourished.

Conditions in the Spalding area proved perfect for growing all types of bulbs. Production began at the end of the 19th Century, with small plots of snowdrops and daffodils.

Among the early industry pioneers were J T White, with premises on the Sheep Market, Sam and Fred Culpin (Culpin's Close, just off Queen's Road, Spalding, is on the site of their nursery) and Dick Wellband.

The first tulips were grown, on a field scale, between 1905 and 1910.

The tulip, a native of Asia Minor, has a fascinating history. A cargo of tulips arrived in Antwerp in 1562 and by 1578 they were growing in England.

One bizarre period in the tulip's history was between 1634 and 1637, when "Tulipmania" struck Holland. Fortunes were made and lost and a single bulb could make the equivalent of £80,000 in today's terms. The most valuable were those with petals whose colour had become broken or feathered. Ironically, this was caused by a virus introduced to the plant by greenfly.

During the First World War, at a meeting held in The White Swan, on June 20, 1916, Spalding Bulb Growers' and Market Gardeners' Association

Horace Braybrooks and staff cropping tulips between the wars.

was formed to co-ordinate the production of food as part of the war effort.

Among those elected to office were Messrs Wellband, Dearnly, Slooten and Baxter.

After the Great War, the association represented the growers' interests locally and nationally and organised shows for fruit, vegetables, daffodils and forced flowers.

Tulip and daffodil "forcing" started around 1920 and is the method of growing flowers in the middle of winter. Boxes are filled with soil (nowadays peat or even just water), and then planted with bulbs. These are then chilled (to fool them into thinking they have had winter), either outside or, more commonly in cold stores.

Tulipmania hits Spalding in 1957, as Tulip Queen Norma Foulsham and her attendants
leave the White Hart Hotel greeted by hoards of well-wishers.

They are then brought into glasshouses and watered and the temperature
raised (they now think it's spring). When the flowers have been cropped the
next filling (or round) is brought in and the sequence repeated.

It was not until very recently that fresh flowers could be flown into this
country from all over the world at any time of year. So for 50 years forced
tulips and daffodils were virtually the only colour available in winter. As a
consequence, the bulb growing and forcing industry expanded rapidly.

An example of the demand for forced flowers occurred when Horace
Braybrooks built his first glasshouse in Cowbit in 1930.

The first winter he put three rounds of tulips through. The first round

Hundreds of people gathered to watch 1957 Tulip Queen Norma Foulsham, of Long Sutton, follow tradition by visiting the tulip fields in and around South Holland. Here she was captured on a visit at Grooms.

paid for the glasshouse, including the boiler and pipework, the second round paid for the bulbs and the third round was profit.

This burgeoning industry in the Fens of south Lincolnshire had not gone unnoticed across the North Sea and it was the Dutch supply of bulbs that largely fuelled the growing and forcing industries.

As late as the 1970s, at certain times of year, the bars of the White Hart and Red Lion Hotels would echo to the voices of Dutch bulb salesmen (as personally researched by the author).

Some of them were not content with just selling bulbs and decided to settle in Spalding.

People came from far and wide to view the vibrant tulip fields which South Holland is now famous for. This picture taken in 1957 shows cars and stalls lining the tulip route.

Slootens, of Cowbit Road, were among the earliest and Do (Dominicus van) Konynenberg started the Spalding Bulb Company, whose huge nursery used to cover an area from the Hawthorn Bank level crossing to Horseshoe Road. His home, Hawthorn House, still stands.

Other influential Dutch names include Moerman, Nell, Goemans and Peter Buschman, whose business Hortico was on Low Road, opposite The Birds pub.

Martin Walkers, another Dutchman, worked for O A Taylor, of Holbeach, and then joined Horace Braybrooks.

Martin's son Johnny is still a well-known name in the industry, regularly winning prizes at Chelsea Flower Show for daffodil displays within the O A Taylor organisation.

But the best-known names of all must be those of John and Len van Geest. John arrived here in 1930, aged 24, and Len in 1938, aged 23. The Geest business was formed in 1930.

One of their earliest nurseries was at Fulney, where Flower Plus is now based. Geest's head office was a near derelict warehouse on Albion Street, which was converted into White House Chambers, an address that became famous around the world. Although Geest was well-known for bananas, its roots were firmly in bulb and other produce growing and marketing.

There were also other local growers, including F H Bowser, Eric Casson, G Bateman, Len Braybrooks, Matthew Dearnly, Fred D'Alcorn, Alf Cunnington and T R Pick.

In March 1932 the *Lincolnshire Free Press* reported that 500 boxes of daffodils a day were being loaded onto the railways in Spalding and the villages for export to Berlin.

In 1933 there were 150 bulb growers in the area and 2,500 acres of bulbs.

This colourful spring display of tulips, daffodils and even hyacinths was becoming quite a spectacle for visitors.

In 1934, the *Lincolnshire Free Press* reported that: "The zenith of flower publicity" was reached when 500 visitors were met by Spalding and District Bulb Growers' Association stewards at Spalding Railway Station and taken on a guided bus tour of the tulip fields.

Because of the increasing amount of tourist chaos on the roads, Mr Hewison, superintendant of the Royal Automobile Club (RAC) and Mr Frank Parsons, deputy clerk to the council, "decided to do something about it" and a Tulip Route was organised.

Plans of the one-way route were printed in the *Spalding Guardian* and *Lincolnshire Free Press* and signposts erected by the RAC to direct motorists on the best routes to see the tulip fields.

By 1939 the bulb acreage had reached 7,500.

But then came the Second World War, and again, as in the First World War, with German U-boats threatening supplies, the priority became food production. The bulb acreage was cut by about 75 per cent, with bulbs largely being grown in orchards and gardens.

There is one mention in the *Lincolnshire Free Press*, on August 5, 1940, under the headline, "Bulbs for Guns", of Geest loading bulbs at Spalding Railway Station for export to the USA.

The van Geest brothers had been caught out by the German invasion of Holland. Both were in this country at the time, John on leave from the Dutch Army and Len having not long been engaged. Len and his fiancee went through the war not knowing whether the other was alive.

After the war, the bulb industry and agriculture generally began to pick up again. The sheep pens had disappeared from the Sheep Market and, along with cattle sales, moved to a new cattle market, between the railway station and Winfrey Avenue.

The Purcell Brothers, of Ireland, brought so many bullocks to Spalding to be fattened by local farmers that they had a full-time representative, John Bergen, living in either the Red Lion or White Hart Hotels.

In 1946 Richard Longstaff established Spalding Bulb and Produce Auction. In 1948 he was joined by Messrs White, Kingston and Tateson.

Although the railways had handled all the millions of boxes of flowers over the years, road haulage companies began to appear. Surfleet farmer George Machin came by two former Army lorries, in payment of a bad debt, along with a driver, Jack Garn. Their first load was of J and L K and H K Braybrooks' flowers from Cowbit to Covent Garden Market.

That was the roundabout beginnings of today's Fowler Welch.

The other main hauliers were Grounds Transport, of Cradge Bank, Parkers, of Surfleet, Fletchers Transport, of Holbeach, and Spalding Haulage, founded by Don Beecham, who had started as a coal merchant. That company became BOC Spalding and is today Gist.

Flowers were the chief loads but they carried all kinds of produce as well.

Paul Hart's Show Garden at Little London. The River Welland can be seen in the top right hand corner and the BP Garage in the bottom right.

Guests from Spalding's twin town of Speyer, in Germany, enjoy a visit to
Paul Hart's show garden.

As the acreage of bulbs returned to its pre-war level, so did the public
interest. British Pathe News, as far back as 1937, had filmed the tulip fields
for showing in cinemas and after the war became regular visitors.

Paul Hart, an RAF pilot, who had been badly burned during the war and
was one of pioneer plastic surgeon Archie MacIndoe's "guinea pigs", came
to Spalding and started a bulb business.

He opened a show garden near Little London Bridge on the corner of
London Road and Hawthorn Bank, which attracted hundreds of visitors a
day during the bulb season.

But Paul's main claim to fame came when Wilfred Pickles interviewed him during a broadcast of the popular radio programme 'Have A Go', from Spalding Corn Exchange.

Wilfred asked Paul how the bulb business was going.

Paul replied that he could do with a few more customers.

Wilfred added: "There you go listeners. The address is Paul Hart, Spalding."

The following Monday the national press was full of reports that Wilfred Pickles had advertised on the BBC and Paul's wife Vera had two sacks of bulb orders to deal with.

In 1951 the press reported a visit by Vera Lynn to Paul Hart and in 1953 an edition of 'Country Magazine' was broadcast live from The Red Lion Hotel. Add all this publicity to the public's increasing ability and desire to travel after the deprivations of the war, and it is clear why Spalding became such a popular destination.

On May 9, 1949, the *Lincolnshire Free Press* reported that the previous Tulip Sunday had seen 100,000 visitors to the area and vehicles were nose to tail around the 34-mile Tulip Route.

All around the route, growers would set up stalls selling flowers and produce, villagers would sell refreshments and churches would be decorated with flowers.

There were also tulip mosaics, which were made using the waste product of tulip bulb growing - the flower heads. These were removed to concentrate the plant's energy into the production of a bulb, rather than a seed pod, and to reduce fungal disease, such as "tulip fire."

One of the most popular mosaics was one by Spalding Parish Church, which was best viewed from the church tower.

The Vespa Club on New Road in an early parade.

One of the many beautiful tulip mosaics outside Spalding's Sessions House, which was one
of many dotted around the area at this time of year.

On two weekends in May 1951 Spalding and District Young Farmers'
Club presented an exhibition in Spalding Bulb Auction Hall to inform visitors
about the bulb and flower growing industry and the history of the tulip.

The Tulip Time Committee was formed to try and co-ordinate events
around Spalding and several different organisations were represented,
including growers, The Urban District Council, The Rural District Council,
East Elloe Council, St John Ambulance and The Royal Automobile Club.

They organised window dressing competitions, The Tulip Route and the
Tulip Queen Competition. Miss Joan Roberts was crowned the first Tulip
Queen in 1950.

On May 5, 1950, the *Lincolnshire Free Press* reported that the town had been so full of people wanting to see the Tulip Queen that 38 policemen and 63 special constables had been required to control the crowds. The Tulip Queen had toured the tulip fields in a decorated coach and The Corn Exchange had been turned into a restaurant.

Originally the Tulip Queen was required to work in the industry but that was not a problem considering how many people the industry employed. In 1958 the Tulip Queen was Janet Bray, the first married woman and mother to be chosen for the title.

After several years of the queen touring the tulip fields in coaches and even a hearse, Janet was the first Tulip Queen to travel on a float made by Geest Industries using the back of a lorry.

In 1945 Spalding and District Bulb Growers' and Market Gardeners'

Traffic nose-to-tail on Cowbit Bank on a Tulip Sunday. Cowbit Wash on the left is still partially flooded.

Association had joined the National Farmers' Union (NFU) and had become South Holland Horticultural Association.

Members had continued to represent growers' interests, organise flower shows, sell half-priced bulbs to the council for Ayscoughfee Gardens, Spalding, and supply free flowers to the town's Johnson Hospital.

They had also supported the Tulip Time Committee and regularly entertained the press and in 1954 The Worshipful Company of Gardeners were guests.

On June 23, 1958, according to the minutes of South Holland Horticultural Association, a meeting was held involving representatives of the association, the NFU and the Tulip Time Committee. It was decided to form a joint sub-committee that "could organise events to stimulate the interest of the national press and television coverage." Among the suggestions were a national flower arrangement competition or "a parade of decorated floats."

In July 1958 the first meeting of the publicity sub-committee of South Holland Horticultural Association was held. Involved were Dick Heath, Horace Braybrooks, Eric Casson, Len van Geest, Cliff Vivian and Francis Hanson, who was elected

The panel at The Red Lion Hotel, Spalding for the live BBC broadcast of "Country Magazine" on Sunday April 26, 1953. Taking part were, Philip Robinson (Presenter), Mr A H Smith, Mr J Levett (Canners), Miss Jean Lambert (Tulip Queen), Mr E C Tavener (Land Drainage), Mr H K Braybrooks (Farmer and Bulb Grower) and Mr A G Moore (Sugar Beet Factory).

chairman. It was agreed that "some form of spectacle was necessary" and it was decided that "the spectacle should take the form of a procession of floats".

The date for the parade was set for May 9, 1959. It was agreed the parade should be the responsibility of South Holland Horticultural Association and the Tulip Time Committee should be responsible for all other arrangements.

Do (pronounced dough) Konynenberg, Percy Taylor and W H White would be co-opted onto the committee and Len van Geest agreed to get more information from Holland about organising a parade.

At a meeting on September 3, officers of the NFU in attendance were Cliff Vivian, Bertie Wray and Ron Hackford, all of whom were to play a large role in years to come. Len van Geest reported to the meeting that he had met Adrianus van Driel, who had designed similar parades in Holland, Germany and Ireland.

It was estimated that the cost of each float, even with free tulip heads and labour, would be between £500 and £600. Due to the cost, it was suggested that maybe just one joint industry float would be all they could do at this stage but it was agreed that Francis Hanson, Horace Braybrooks and Cliff Vivian would approach other potential sponsors.

On September 22 it was agreed to invite Mr van Driel to design floats for the Tulip Queen and the industry "to advertise Lincolnshire grown bulbs and flowers". Mr van Driel insisted on full control as he had "an international reputation to consider."

Spalding and District Young Farmers wished to enter a float and the Tulip Time Committee wanted to enter decorated cars.

On January 8 it was agreed to call the carnival "The Flower Parade."

At subsequent meetings, the minutes reported that radio vans would be

Horace Braybrooks with Mary Battley (née Walkers) on Goemans' float in front of the
Cattle Market Offices before the 1959 parade.

used, Peterborough Pipe Band and Kirton Town Band would participate, St.
John Ambulance would provide teas for participants, and Reg Rowell, of
Geest, would supervise the construction of floats. A £250 grant was obtained
from the Flower Publicity Council.

On May 9, 1959, the first Flower Parade took to the streets of Spalding.
It consisted of floats, decorated cars, bands and even the local Vespa club.

As well as The Tulip Queen's float and the industry float, there were floats
from Butlins, Smedley's, Elsoms, Goemans and the Young Farmers' Club.

On May 12 the *Lincolnshire Free Press* called it a "Great triumph for
growers in a courageous experiment," and announced: "At the first attempt,
this area has firmly established itself in the forefront of the world in the art
of floral presentation."

The Early Years

A handful of growers, with the help of the local branch of the National Farmers' Union and a Dutch designer, had put on a show at their first attempt which would soon be famous around the world.

Organisers agreed that the first parade had been an enormous success but they set about making improvements for the next one. Over the first few years many changes took place before a routine emerged which would remain virtually unchanged for 30 years.

The original purpose of the parade was to promote the local bulb and flower industry and organisers went to great lengths to entertain the local, national and international press. In 1960, committee members Gerard Nell and Dick Heath met journalists at Peterborough Railway Station and travelled with them to Spalding.

After that parade some in the industry were disappointed at the lack of coverage in the national dailies. But the parade had featured on the BBC and ITV and reports appeared in the African and Commonwealth press.

Even so, several industry members doubted the value of the parade. Some growers were slow in their support and enthusiasm in the town was patchy.

The Spalding Salvation Army Band in Bridge Street, during an early parade. Note that the road was still open to two-way traffic.

In 1963 concern was again expressed about the lack of community support and it was stated that: "It was desirable that the public should be brought into the centre of Spalding, but in turn, Spalding must provide a worthy attraction."

Many town businesses did support the parade by entering floats, sponsoring bands or just giving cash and there were always volunteers willing to pin tulip heads on floats.

The official programme was also regarded as a very important tool in advertising the industry and Bill Barnacle, of Geest Industries, was put in charge.

The programme gave visitors information about the route and parade times as well as bulb and flower industry facts and useful tips for the gardener and flower arranger.

The 1962 programme introduction read: "Spalding Flower Parade will, we hope, serve to remind you of the colour and beauty of the bulbs and flowers which we grow. And perhaps, too, it will help you to bear in mind that we, in Lincolnshire, can grow bulbs as good as any other farmers in the world - and probably better."

The head of an early parade in New Road.

After this, one could have understood if organisers wondered if they were wasting their time when one of them was asked by a visiting VIP: "How much does it cost to bring all these tulip heads over from Holland?"

It is interesting to note that if it was a particularly early or late season, the organisers were prepared to alter the dates of early parades. In 1963, after a

Pam Braybrooks beside her father's decorated Humber Hawk just before it represented the Flower Publicity Council in the first Flower Parade.

very cold winter, the parade was put back a full two weeks to May 18. With all the pre-booking of coaches, excursion trains and bands, this would have been unthinkable a few years later.

The early floats were designed by Adrianus van Driel, but he was soon joined by his son Kees, who eventually took over the work.

A Vauxhall of Wellband passes Campion's Rootes Group Garage in New Road, where The Ivy Wall now stands, during the 1960 parade.

For several years, Geest Industries built its own and the Tulip Queen's float, the rest being built by the sponsors themselves or by blacksmiths employed by them. Later Spalding blacksmith Geoff Dodd was building almost all of the floats.

From early on the floats were dressed and finished at the Bulb Auction Halls, but work to pin on the heads did not start until the day before each parade because of fears that the tulip heads would not last over the weekend.

It had been suggested that tulip heads should be supplied with a two-inch stem, picked early or late in the day and packed in wooden flower boxes. It was gradually discovered that the two-inch stem was a nuisance, the time of day made no difference, the best receptacle for tulip heads was a plastic fertiliser bag and that tulip heads could be cold-stored.

By 1964, Mr van Driel was so impressed by the high standard of workmanship by float builders and dressers that he allowed for much more intricate designs.

Originally the parade formed and returned to the cattle market, with very little opportunity for public viewing of static floats so in 1962 it was decided to use the Sir Halley Stewart Field for this purpose.

This move proved to be "eminently justified," though it was agreed that "this should be a proper production, rather than just a dumping ground for floats."

National Farmers' Union (NFU) agent Ron Hackford was in charge of organising the field. Spalding Young Farmers' Club asked if members could provide catering facilities and it was decided that the NFU should put on an agricultural display.

There was even a suggestion that the council should be approached about

Crowds in New Road.

using the field as a more permanent show garden, because, someone claimed, "football seemed to be dying a natural death."

As we now know, the football continued and the show garden was built a few years later at Fulney and was called Springfields.

The only permanent change to the field was a road around the perimeter, with the Flower Parade committee contributing half of the £600 cost. This was in addition to the rent, which by 1966 had reached £100.

The number of people wishing to see the static display of floats began to overwhelm the existing facilities on the Sir Halley Stewart Field.

The turnstiles could not admit people quickly enough so new cashier huts were hired from The East of England Show Society before the committee

Orderly crowds fill Hall Place and the roof of Pennington's shop, now Boots.

bought its own. These were manned by volunteers from the National Farmers' Union offices.

In 1963, it was decided to extend the exhibition of floats to cover Saturday, Sunday, Monday and Tuesday. The parade itself was, of course, a free show, but costs had to be covered somehow.

There were four main ways.

Firstly, the growers who provided the majority of the labour put in no bill. Nor did the NFU staff.

Secondly, there was the gate money from the Sir Halley Stewart Field.

Thirdly, the float sponsors. Originally, as well as their building costs, sponsors were charged a designer's fee and an entry fee, although the entry fee was waived for association members.

Standard bearers from Spalding Young Farmers enter the Market Place in the first parade.

Lastly, money was raised from the sale of the programmes, which were originally sold by Spalding Round Table.

In 1960 Francis Hanson suggested a street collection but this was ruled out at the time. Local traders were also asked for financial support in 1960, with limited results, although the parade had some loyal, long term supporters in the town.

It was pointed out in 1968 that "there was, as yet, no actual profit" from the parade and that if growers started charging for labour, there would be a deficit. It was also pointed out that there was "no call on National Farmers' Union funds and "that all staff ran the parade on a voluntary basis."

The parade was marshalled from radio vans by members of the Civil Defence and in 1962 they were described by the organisers as "very co-operative and doing an excellent job." They carried on doing the job until 1968, when the police took over.

Despite their best efforts, however, there was still the perennial problem of crowd control and gaps in the parade, which were blamed on the photographers and the bands.

As if predicting parades in 40 years' time, it was suggested that bands

Elsoms' float in the Market Place, with the Corn Exchange in the background.

might be put on "some form of conveyance." Taped music on the floats, though, was described as "unsuccessful."

The first parades used a shorter route than was to be the norm and went in the opposite direction to today's parades.

They left Winfrey Avenue, then went along King's Road, Pinchbeck Road, New Road, Hall Place, Market Place, over High Bridge, along Churchgate, Love Lane, Halmergate, Queen's Road, Holbeach Road, over West Elloe Bridge, along West Elloe Avenue, Pinchbeck Road, King's Road and Winfrey Avenue.

In 1963 the police estimated that 175,000 people had watched the parade. That figure was to be more than doubled in years to come.

By the mid 1960s, the bulb industry around Spalding was huge. There were 4,000 acres of daffodils and 3,000 acres of tulips. There were 130 acres of glass for forcing and 25,000 boxes of flowers left Spalding every day. The industry employed 12,000 people at a time when the urban population of Spalding was 15,000.

Geest became the biggest single grower in the area with 600 acres of daffodils and 250 acres of tulips and 1,000 tons of forced daffodils a year. Geest acquired the Spalding Bulb Company, J T White's and Hortico and at one time sent out bulb catalogues in seven different names.

Jim Horberry, general manager of the bulb division at the time, recalls once buying 100 acres of a single variety of tulip (Rose Copeland) from T R Pick, of Whaplode. Another big player was Lingarden, the Weston-based growers' co-operative.

After the 1961 parade, the chairman Horace Braybrooks called it: "An outstanding success" and expressed his satisfaction at what had been achieved in the three years since the parade began.

Crowds gathered on the opposite side of the river outside Berrills department store where
the parade was due to pass in 1966.

Not only was the standard greatly improved but, to his mind, there was
a greater atmosphere of co-operation and friendliness shown by members. It
was this co-operation and friendliness that was to keep the parade going
when its future began to look in doubt.

The Sir Halley Stewart Years – The Organisation

The Parade Committee was a sub-committee of South Holland Horticultural Association, a specialist branch of the National Farmers' Union (NFU).

Committee members were not necessarily association members but some were co-opted because of contributions they could make, like Gordon Cummins, of P M Tractors, who served on the committee for years.

The parade officers were originally secretaries with the NFU. Cliff Vivian was county secretary and was heavily involved with organising early parades, along with his assistant Jean Pamley.

Two other NFU secretaries/agents who were an important part of the parade were Bertie Wray (float dressing) and Ron Hackford (float exhibition on the Sir Halley Stewart Field) who operated from offices at Elsom House, Broad Street, Spalding.

Attending a South Holland Horticultural Association meeting in 1964 was Percy Taylor's son John, who was on work experience. He later became Lord Taylor of Holbeach and chairman of Springfields Council.

When Cliff Vivian left the NFU he was replaced as county secretary by Bill Hunt, who also played his part supporting the parade.

The bulk of the work then fell to Jean Pamley, who later operated from Springfields. She was replaced by float designer Kees van Driel, who she later married, and he then took a more important administrative role, as well as continuing to design the floats.

In 1976 Peter Atkinson replaced Kees and became general manager of Springfields, which included responsibility for the gardens, Springfields Horticultural Exhibition, Spalding Flower Parade, and bulb and flower publicity generally.

Kees, Jean and their family then emigrated to Australia, but Kees continued to design the floats from there.

Over the years at Springfields, there were loyal office staff including Joyce Basing, Karen Gerrard (née Mayfield) and Rosemary Pilgrim.

These officers would attend meetings of South Holland Horticultural Association and then Springfields Council and the Flower Parade Committee. Then staff would set about attracting sponsors, booking bands, taking coach bookings, finding tractors to go under floats, organising labour, answering inquiries and doing all the other jobs that staging an event of this scale requires.

Floats and Sponsors

Adrianus, and then Kees van Driel were given a theme to work to, or they would suggest one themselves. They would come up with designs that committee members would offer to firms and organisations in the hope that they might sponsor a float.

Len van Geest was particularly good at persuading some of the larger companies that they ought to have a float in Spalding Flower Parade. Kees later took over this promotion work and then Peter Atkinson.

Many sponsors had their own themes or logos that they wanted to incorporate. For example, Turners Turkeys always wanted turkeys on its float, which were very time consuming to build, and John Player and Sons often wanted to bring attention to whatever they were sponsoring that year, such as a Formula One racing team.

The Geest float in 1982, with the ship represented on their float, on its way to the Falklands War.

Thomas the Tank Engine in 1995.

Kees sometimes had to work very closely with the sponsor before coming up with a design that was both practical to make and acceptable to them. Colour could be a problem. For example, the black of a John Player Special racing car would have been difficult to guarantee.

The organisations that sponsored floats ranged from villages to a global brewer, from a local club to a national supermarket and from a small grower to a high street bank.

There were basically two sizes of floats. Singles, which were one unit built around a tractor, and doubles, which were the same but towing a trailer unit as well.

A magnificent Midland Bank tiger loose in Springfields, after the 1974 Parade.

The designs took the form of a watercolour sketch.

This process needed to begin several months before the parade to allow the builder and cladder time to construct all of the floats.

Kees enjoyed a feeling of movement and there was often humour in his designs. There were plenty of animals and cartoon-like characters.

Wherever possible, fresh designs were used every year, except for the Tulip Queen's float, which was sometimes used more than once to keep the cost to the council down and to reduce the blacksmith's workload.

Some figures such as horses, turkeys and even polar bears could be salvaged and re-used.

In 1958 the cost of a float was estimated at £500-£600, but, a few years later, £15,000 could be paid for a large, spectacular float.

Once a sponsor had chosen a design, Kees could then prepare a working drawing for the blacksmith to build the float.

Players' float in 1969.

Lock, Stock and Barrel. Pinchbeck Village float in 1969.

Construction of Floats

Spalding blacksmith Geoff Dodd, who started float building in 1960 and retired in 2003, had a hand in building more parade floats than anybody in Spalding.

He built his first float for Mr Keller, of Stassens, in 1960. In 1961, he also built Interflora's and the GPO's (the Post Office), and by the late 1960s he was building most of the floats.

When Kees or Peter had found a sponsor for a particular design, Kees would provide a detailed drawing, from which Geoff could take accurate measurements, enabling him to build exactly what Kees had in mind.

Sometimes Geoff would project the plan onto cardboard to give him a template from which to work. The shapes of the floats and the figures on the

A striking Lowland Bulb Company float in 1969.

floats were made by cutting, bending and welding lengths of mild steel around a more substantial steel frame.

Work would usually start on building the floats at the beginning of November, and though it took 14 hours a day, seven days a week, Geoff still found time to fulfil his commitment as a Methodist Lay Preacher on a Sunday evening.

Geoff did have some part-time help but he had many long and lonely hours in often cold and draughty sheds in the middle of winter.

In 1982, he worked 1,386 hours building floats, with the casual help putting in 962 hours, in which time they completed 16 floats, ten of which were doubles.

"Diddymen" in 1969.

A single unit float would take about 100 hours to make. A large double could take up to 250 hours.

In an average year Geoff was using up to 14 miles of steel, 7,000 welding rods and 140,000 welds to produce a parade.

A single float would be 24ft long by about 12ft wide but a double could be up to 60ft long. Height was restricted by the door at No.4 shed at the Bulb Auction (12ft) and overhead wires and bunting around the route of the parade (16ft).

To make the most of the discrepancy between the two heights, many of the higher parts of the floats were made removable, such as hats, heads, signs, flags and flower arrangements and were added once the floats were out of the shed.

Gleed School girls in 1969.

For the first couple of years, Geoff built his floats at his blacksmith's shop on the High Street, Spalding, actually putting them together in the road outside.

Later, as he was making more and more, it became a problem finding sheds where he could continue to build and store floats from November through to May.

Gordon Cummins, Geoff Dodd, Pete Bell and helpers put a tractor under an already constructed and strawed float.

Over the years, he found himself working in all sorts of sheds, some of which were better suited to the job than others. Some had no sides and to find a heated one was an absolute luxury. To begin with the sheds were made available, free of charge, by generous growers and others.

Venues included Ted Law's, White House Chambers, Lingarden, Brian Drury's, and Gee Tee Bulb Company.

One job that is often forgotten is that of dismantling the floats when the show was over. This also fell to Geoff, and it too had to be paid for.

Tractors

Each float required a power unit, almost always an agricultural tractor. They needed to be small, to allow the float to be built around them. Ford Dexters and Massey Ferguson 135s were ideal.

Murgatroyd the Magpie, entered by Thames Television.

The Spalding Guardian celebrates its Centenary, in 1981, with a float based on its logo at the time. Ayscoughfee Owl

A dynamic and aromatic float, entered by British Rail, to celebrate the introduction of the Inter-City 125. As well as using locally produced tulip and daffodil heads, highly scented hyacinths were

As tractors could not be tied up for more than a few days, especially in the spring, the float was usually built first and then the tractor was driven in and the rear of the float put in place, completely encasing the tractor.

Often tractors had to be modified, with exhaust systems realigned and mudguards removed.

To begin with, most of the tractors were supplied by growers but as this supply became less reliable, other sources had to be found.

Gordon Cummins, of Motors and Tractors (which became P M Tractors), came to the rescue. He also provided the forklift and teleporter (with driver) for use in the field for all the high work.

When safety cabs were introduced, finding tractors without them became more difficult but Gordon had some diverted between the factory and the

Tulip heads, laurel leaves, palms, material and flower arrangements, make a big impact with this float of Adams.

docks to have a short stay in Spalding before continuing on their journey to countries where such safety concerns were not compulsory.

Small tractors, of the sort required to go under floats, became harder to come by so the organisers decided to buy their own.

This task fell to Cowbit grower and committee member Stuart Gibbard, now the editor of an international tractor magazine.

Stuart's remit was to go to farm sales and pick up, at the best possible price, suitable tractors. The age of the tractors meant that he often had to repair and service them to a standard that would hopefully see them getting

The Potato Marketing Board float in the 1965 parade.

round the parade route without mishap. Due to his knowledge and skill, those tractors performed well for many years. In fact, one or two may still be operating now.

Cladding

After Geoff had made the frames, rye straw matting was used to allow the tulip heads to be attached. This was usually used for rolling out on the outside of glasshouses to provide shade from the sun in the summer.

It was bought from the Continent by the container load.

The highly skilled work of fixing the straw matting to the steel framework was in the hands of Pete Bell. Pete used nylon string and an old fashioned sack

Pinchbeck West Village horse-drawn float in 1964.

needle to sew the matting onto Geoff's steel shapes, having first cut them to shape and size, using hand sheep shears.

The straw mats were 10ft by 6ft and about 26 were required per float, meaning up to 500 could be required each year.

This work was also time consuming and began as soon as Geoff had finished building the first float. Pete worked alongside Geoff in the same cold sheds. Later he was helped by his son Richard.

The price of the matting went up and organisers had to look for another material. It had to be soft enough to allow the attachment of a pin but robust enough to hold onto that pin as it shook its way around the town.

The ideal replacement was found in the form of polythene foam sheeting, which was easily glued to the frame and was much cheaper and far less time consuming. This work was done by Springfields staff, including Michael Pratt.

The foam sheeting was not without its teething troubles. One Sunday morning, float dressing supervisor Gordon Scott received a wake-up call from Bertie Wray, from the Sir Halley Stewart Field.

After heavy rain the floats were collapsing under the weight of water. A sharp knife and some repair work solved the immediate problem and Gordon made sure it did not happen again.

Parade Run-up

In the week before the parade, things really started to get busy.

Staff mainly employed by Len and Horace Braybrooks started bringing equipment out of storage, using tractors and trailers. For many years this was at Magpie Holt Farm at Weston Hills.

Ticket kiosks had to be taken to the Sir Halley Stewart Field and erected.

A lot of white tulip heads were needed to dress this Olau Line float.

Hundreds of crowd control barriers had to be taken to the major junctions along the parade route.

One of the most awkward and time-consuming jobs was the erection of a large, steel-framed sign that straddled the Winfrey Avenue entrance to the exhibition of floats, with deep post holes having to be dug, by hand, every year.

Trestles, planks and pins were taken to the cattle market.

By the Wednesday before parade day tulip heads were brought in by growers.

Marquees and stands were being erected on the Sir Halley Stewart Field to accommodate exhibitors and caterers.

Changing fashions, as shown by young ladies from the NFU and also opposite.

Electricity was laid on by local electrician Robert Bowman.

On the Wednesday evening float drivers and other volunteers would assemble at the Bulb Auction and be taken to wherever the floats had been built that year.

The floats would then be driven, usually in convoy, with a police escort, to the No. 4 shed. As the floats arrived (in a predetermined order) they were put into place by Bertie Wray. No sooner had the floats been parked than the trestles and planks required for dressing the high work were put into place ready for a good start the next morning.

After the parade weekend, the same staff needed to clear up and put all the signs and kiosks back into storage.

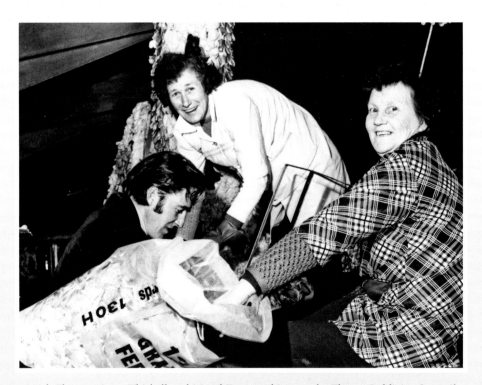

Mick Flowers, Lucy Thirkell and Maud Fear working on the Flower Publicity Council float. Notice the 1cwt fertilizer bag which was the container of choice for storing and handling tulip heads.

Dressing The Floats

First thing on the Thursday morning, No. 4 shed became a hive of activity.

Bertie Wray had different gangs of labour designated to different floats. Several sponsors decorated their own floats but several national companies needed the expertise of an experienced labour force.

Local growers provided the bulk of the workers and float supervisors.

At a Flower Parade Committee meeting in 1978, Bertie asked for more supervisors, listing the current ones as Rodney Houghton, Doug Braybrooks, J Cooke, P Mills, Mick Flowers and Mrs Matthews.

Volunteers busy themselves attaching every single tulip head by hand in preparation for the 1961 parade.

First job for the supervisors was to make sure that there were sufficient tulip heads of any particular colour to cover a given area. It was no good getting half a figure covered only to discover that a colour had run out.

Then staff were shown where to start and with what colour. Experienced ones were left to it, while newcomers were shown how to pin on heads.

The colours that Kees had chosen were not always available in sufficient quantities. White and especially black were often in short supply. Len

Parade Marshals assemble on the Sir Halley Stewart Field, before a parade. Adrian Chappell, Doug Braybrooks, Charles Dobney and Adrian Jansen.

Braybrooks grew Queen of the Night tulips in the hope that there would at least be enough black for the pupils of the figures' eyes.

Wire pins, about four inches long and imported from Germany, were used to fix on the heads. They were bent double to form two prongs with very sharp points. The pin was pushed through the base of the tulip, at a 45 degree angle, then through the straw or plastic sheeting.

It had to be pressed home far enough to hold firm but not so hard that it crushed the tulip. Work started, wherever possible, at the bottom of the area being covered, with the stalks pointing upwards, pinning on a row at a time.

Then the next row would be added, with the petals of the second row covering the pin and stalks of the first, and so on, in the same way as putting tiles on a roof.

Small buds, tightly packed, could give a very neat finish, but were very time consuming and required a lot of heads. Large, mature heads could cover a large area very quickly, but could look untidy and may not last over the whole weekend.

A large float could take 100,000 to 200,000 heads to cover it, each one pinned on individually.

Geest staff dressed their own float and helped out on several others. If work was falling behind, Len van Geest would send extra buses of female staff to get things back on track.

J T White's staff dressed the Tulip Queen's float for several years.

Horace Braybrooks' staff worked on the Flower Publicity Council float and helped with Geo Adams' float. The whole family, and several enthusiastic members of staff, would get involved with the Geo Adams float and Caroline Goodwin (née Adams), and Suzie Edwards were particularly imaginative with

Fiddly work in 1961: each tulip head is attached to the straw frames using a pin. Each one has to be in the right place, the right way round and the right colour!

their use of alternative coverings, with Kermit the Frog dressed with laurel leaves and seals covered with moss.

Other long-serving suppliers of labour were Tom Maxey, of Groom Bros, and O A Taylor, under the supervision of long-term committee member Brian Taylor. The Young Farmers' Club and Lingarden dressed their own floats.

The other main source of labour were groups raising money for charity, including Bourne Abbey Young Wives, the Air Training Corps, Deeping St. Nicholas Women's Institute, The Lions, Oxfam and Holbeach Wives.

Pete Bell strawing a float, in 1978.

One of the hundreds of volunteers holding one of the millions of pins used to secure the tulip head.

Eventually, as the acreage of tulips declined along with the number of people employed in the industry, more and more gang labour was used, until almost all of the float workers were paid out of flower parade funds.

One of the earliest gangers was Derek Jarvis, of Eye Green, Peterborough, who also had a float in the parade for a few years.

There was almost a party atmosphere in the shed. Everyone wanted their float to look the best but would help another float out if they were finished early.

In the evenings, Bertie would organise sandwiches in The Chequers pub, and he, some of the float supervisors, some committee members and other supporters would adjourn there, either to celebrate a job well done or as a break before continuing the work.

Sometimes more difficult floats would not be finished until the early hours of Saturday morning.

When Bertie Wray retired, Gordon Scott, of Groom Bros, an experienced float supervisor, took charge of dressing all of the floats.

As well as tulip heads, all sorts of other accoutrements had to be attached, such as signs, flags, voile, material and grass matting.

NFU members in conversation with members of the public.

The Farm Workers' Union, (The NUAW), entered this float,
"The Happy Worker", in 1964.

A tulip head mosaic in 1963. Many clubs and villages entered mosaics into competitions.

Usually, the finishing touch to a float would be flower arrangements. Sometimes this would be done by the sponsor's own florist but, more often than not, this final flourish was provided by members of Spalding Flower Lovers' Club.

Flower Lovers' Club

The Flower Lovers' Club was formed by growers' wives and friends. Two of the founder members were Lucy Saunders and Madge Nell. Each year they would take responsibility for the flower arrangements for most of the floats.

In 1981, Barbara Drury bought flowers for 125 separate arrangements. The amounts required were 375 stems of spray carnations, 375 stems of single carnations, 375 stems of stocks, 500 stems of spray chrysanthemums,

George Adams' staff, busy selling their pork products, on The Sir Halley Stewart Field.

Miss Tulipland Sharon Holmes, with Deputy Miss Tulipland Joanne Allen, goes aloft to make her welcome speech on the Sir Halley Stewart Field, accompanied by Doug Braybrooks.

375 stems of iris and 375 bunches of tulips. Colours were co-ordinated to go with each float.

Foliage was collected from Springfields Gardens the night before. Sometimes there could be up to 270 arrangements in the parade.

For several years the flower wholesaler supplying the flowers was Vic Stanberry. Another wholesaler used was Brian Green.

The arrangements were put into special containers mounted on the float, at the time of construction, by Geoff.

About 50 ladies started work on the Friday morning, often not finishing until the early hours of Saturday morning. It was sometimes difficult working around staff who were still pinning on heads in a confined space. Many of these ladies also did arrangements for their local church festivals.

The Parade Morning

Work began on parade morning before 6am.

The first priority was to move the floats from No.4 shed to the Sir Halley Stewart Field across the road before the crowds started to arrive.

Most of this work was done by the float drivers, float supervisors and other helpers, some of whom may have finished dressing floats just a few hours before.

Any clearing up of left over tulip heads, trestles and planks that had not been finished the night before had to be done and the whole shed swept ready to receive the bands who would use it to park their coaches and get ready in a few hours' time.

Once the floats were in the field, all the flags, signs, flower arrangements and the heads of figures that were too tall to get out of the shed door had to be put in place using a forklift.

The Fantasy Girls, from Holland, who took part in the 1986 parade, with a goofy friend.

In 1982 a float had gone round the route with the sign that should have been atop the float laying on the back.

After the understandable furore, the chairman Rob Teeuw gave the responsibility of ensuring that all floats were properly finished to Doug Braybrooks.

When all the floats were ready, it became a tradition that Doug would treat anyone who had helped to a bacon butty at John Cresswell's bus station café across the road.

The Parade

The route and start time of the parade altered over the years, often influenced by when and how the police wanted the town emptying afterwards.

Judy, Sarah and Hilary, the three young Adams girls enter Hall Place on the family firm's float.

To begin with it went through the town first, then later went the other way.

One year Love Lane was missed out and it went down Church Street, and when Springfields was opened, the route was extended to include Roman Bank and Camelgate.

The parade could not start without the Tulip Queen, who always attended the civic reception.

Sometimes her arrival in Harry Land's limousine, despite the best efforts of police outriders, would be delayed by the crowds.

Once in the field, she would be raised aloft on the forklift, under the supervision of Doug Braybrooks, to make a welcome speech to the crowds.

She would then be put on her float and when the bands had marched from the Bulb Auction, where they had formed up under the supervision of committee member Adrian van Egmond, and the remaining float riders put in their seats, the parade could begin.

The most crucial components of the parade were the decorated floats but there were many other important participants, first among them the marching bands.

In the early years there were some famous military bands, namely the Band of the Grenadier Guards, the Band of the 1st Battalion, the Parachute Regiment and the United States Air Force Band.

There were colliery bands from Grimethorpe and Markham Main, pipe bands from Peterborough and Stewarts and Lloyds of Corby, bands from Holland, such as the Flora Band and the Avendo Band. Local bands included Kirton Town Band, Swineshead Silver Band, the Salvation Army Band, the British Legion Band and the Church Lads' and the Church Girls' Brigade Band.

Among the longest serving and most popular were Melton Mowbray Tally-Ho Band, the 13th Coventry Scout Group, the Derby Serenaders and the Ely Military Band.

But probably the favourite with the crowds were the Romsey Old Cadets, who would use Spalding Flower Parade to introduce their new comedy costume for the season.

The crowds looked forward to their antics, such as all collapsing on their backs when "shot" by a cannon, which was pulled along just in front of them.

Paraphernalia such as the cannon were also used to (poorly) conceal a barrel of beer which was used for refreshment but resulted in unscheduled visits by the band to households along the route to avail themselves of the

William Rodwell, Banks' Farm Manager, driving Bill Banks' 1922 Rolls Royce Silver Ghost in the 1997 Flower Parade. In the front passenger seat is Gladys Smith, widow of the owner of Snowdrop Nurseries, who had ridden on their 1961 float "The Old Lady Who Lived in a Shoe." Behind is the parade's first ever *Lincolnshire Free Press* and *Spalding Guardian* Prince and Princess, William Reddin and Sally Fulcher with chaperone Julie Bearcock.

facilities. Very amusing for spectators, but it taxed the nerves of the poor marshals who were trying to keep the parade moving.

Other elements of the parade came and went over the years.

Early participants included Spalding Cycling Club and Spalding Vespa

Club and Long Sutton and District Veteran Cycle Club, which is still taking part today.

There were traction engines, veteran cars, vintage fire engines, ponies and traps, police horses, medieval jousters, floats drawn by heavy horses, groups carrying banners, majorettes and open top cars carrying celebrities.

Great care was taken by the parade organisers in selecting parade participants. At a meeting in 1962 it was agreed that: "The parade should be allowed to develop into a carnival but should retain a certain amount of dignity in order to project an image of a solid industry."

It was many a child's dream to get dressed up and be part of the spectacle. Although it was essentially the Tulip Queen's parade, along with her attendants, other beauty queens graced the spectacle.

Miss Yorkshire Television and the John Player Girls were regular visitors, along with Miss Jersey Battle of Flowers, who often rode in Bill Banks' open top 1922 Rolls Royce Silver Ghost.

With sometimes very poor visibility and crowds of spectators and photographers pressing in from all sides, negotiating bottlenecks such as the Love Lane and Church Gate Corner and High Bridge and Bridge Street was a test of nerves and driving skill.

Driving stalwarts include Paul Hackford, David Rutterford, Brian Willson, Jerry Cook, Ted Hancock, "Scrapper" Parkin, Pete Bell and Clive Gotobed.

Clive rode on his first float, at the age of ten, in 1961. He started driving floats at the age of 18 and is still driving.

The breakdown vehicles provided by local garages and agricultural engineers are not just for show - there have been several occasions when floats have finished the parade under tow.

Another familiar sight were programme sellers from Spalding Round Table and then Holbeach Round Table, dressed as minstrels.

At the end of the four mile route, the parade would return to The Sir Halley Stewart Field, with participants either hot and dusty or cold and wet but almost always tired and happy.

They could then go over the road to the Bulb Auction Hall for a reviving cup of tea and a light meal provided by St John Ambulance.

The Floats Exhibition

When the Sir Halley Stewart Field was first used for exhibiting the floats in 1962 Ron Hackford, of the National Farmers' Union (NFU) was the field organiser, until 1979, when Bertie Wray took on the job, helped by Rodney Flowers.

Floats line up in the Sir Halley Stewart Playing Field in 1961 for the first time. Notice the lack of facilities compared to later years.

77

John Player
Carlton
John Player
Carlton
John Player
Carlton
John Player
Carlton

Johnny Walkers, with other Young Farmers, providing refreshments on the Sir Halley Stewart Field, in 1972.

Jim Benton, a Moulton Chapel grower, helped for several years, followed by Stuart Gibbard. Bertie finally retired from being the field organiser in 1989.

The Sir Halley Stewart Field did become more than "just a dumping ground for floats," although the floats were the main attraction. Any company or organisation which sponsored a float was entitled to space for a stand to promote, exhibit or sell their product or service.

George Adams had a large display of its pork products and would do a roaring trade selling sausage rolls and pork pies.

The NFU always had a stand in a marquee, displaying the huge range of crops and resulting products grown by local and British farmers and growers.

CIS sold double glazing and insurance and John Player's young ladies sold cigarettes.

Geest sold a range of its products, sometimes with the help of the Spalding Round Table.

The *Spalding Guardian* and *Lincolnshire Free Press* had a stand, as, for a while, did Yorkshire Television.

The Football Club sold tulips, St. John Ambulance provided First Aid facilities and there were ice cream vans. There was also an arts and crafts marquee.

The biggest marquee on the field, however, was the refreshment tent

Pete Bell, Geoff Dodd and Parade Chairman (1980-1982) Rob Teeuw, surrounded by strawed floats.

staffed by Spalding and District Young Farmers' Club. The Young Farmers had a float in every parade, always building their own.

The refreshment tent was organised like a cafeteria with volunteer young farmers making hundreds of sandwiches. In a good year they would serve up to 14,000 cups of tea.

Possibly the most important stand on the field was the Midland Bank stand. This provided banking facilities for gate money, stand-holders and the public and provided refreshments for their customers but also acted as headquarters for the Flower Parade Committee over the parade weekend.

Alan Bellamy was not only Spalding branch manager for the Midland Bank but also honorary treasurer of the Flower Parade and Springfields. Alan kept a count of gate numbers so that attendances from one year to the next could be compared.

Organisers, with wives and friends, along with senior police officers, would gather on the parade evening to review the day.

On the Sunday there was a photocall and all those who had ridden on floats were put back on to enable the public to take photographs.

As attendances in the field began to fall, more entertainment was laid on in an attempt to attract people in, especially during the parade. This included marching band competitions, falconry and dog obedience demonstrations.

The Tulip Queen

Ever since Joan Roberts became the first Tulip Queen in 1950, the girls chosen to represent the industry and area have been the central figures during Tulip Time. Even before The Flower Parade started, huge crowds would turn out to see them tour the tulip fields. Cinema goers would have watched them and their attendants on Pathe News.

Past Tulip Queens assemble for a reunion in 1988. They include:- 1967 Eileen Favell,
1980 Valerie Whitworth (then White) 1975 Elaine Packard, 1973 Pip Cousins (Lowther),
1966 Dawn Stockdale (Robinson), 1961 Nora Woods (Smith), 1962 June Green
(Nickols), 1968 Elizabeth Barker (Ford), 1964 Joyce Green (Baker), 1960 Wendy Smith
(Nellson), 1950 Joan Roberts (Dalton), 1969 Judith Smith, 1953 Jean Lambert (Tooley),
1986 Helen Cave, 1985 Helen Drake (Fairburn), 1984 Sharon Holmes, 1957 Norma
Foulsham (Hardy), 1983 Wendy Johnson (Revill).

In 1967 the title changed from the Tulip Queen, to Miss Tulipland and
in 1988 she became the Flower Queen.

Queens have represented Spalding in Holland and Jersey, and during their
year in office appeared around the area, opening functions and visiting
hospitals. Over the years different ways have been used to select a suitable girl
to act as ambassador for the area. There have been different venues, too, to
mark the crowning of the Tulip Queen, frequently by celebrities including
Jimmy Savile, Ronnie Carroll and Eric Morecambe.

In 1988 the parade committee organised a reunion of Tulip Queens on the exhibition site on the Sunday, attended by 24 former queens.

The Crowds

In 1963 the police estimated the number of people in Spalding watching the parade, free of charge, at 175,000. By the 1970s, the estimate had risen to almost half a million. The only precise figures available were for ticket sales for the Sir Halley Stewart Field.

In 1971 attendance on the field was 110,000 over the four days.

Coaches and cars would queue for miles on every road into Spalding on parade morning, often further than Cowbit, Surfleet and Pode Hole.

"Beatlemania". Spalding Young Farmers are "with it" in 1964.

Every available parking space in town was utilised, including the Gleed School, High School and Grammar School playing fields, Winfrey Avenue car park, the Cattle Market, the Railway Station Yard and Geest's factory.

To go into Spalding on parade day you had to arrive early, park and forget your car until the evening, when everybody had gone home.

For a few days before the parade caravanners would begin arriving at fields in and around Spalding and every hotel and guesthouse room for miles

Spalding Market Place was jam-packed with crowds out to celebrate the
1966 tulip-time festivities.

around was booked a year in advance. Special excursion trains were also provided from all over the country.

So many people took photographs of the parade that Kodak noticed a distinct increase in demand for their developing service immediately following the event.

All these extra people flooding into the town and outlying villages needed food, refreshment, accommodation, parking and entertainment, and many clubs, churches and other organisations made enough money providing these to finance themselves for the rest of the year.

Some businesses felt that the parade was bad for trade but some of the money that came into the area found its way into their tills over the next few months. A few businesses donated money towards supporting the parade, but some did not.

Some Spalding residents went away for the weekend, while some who had moved away, such as students, returned to enjoy the carnival atmosphere and extended opening hours.

The Police

From the beginning, and especially at the height of its popularity, the parade would not have been possible without the full support, help and co-operation of the Lincolnshire Police.

The parade is a team event and the police were very much a part of that team. They regarded the event as a good public relations exercise and treated it as good training for crowd control on a large scale.

From the beginning, the parade was always led by a police car, although until 1968, it was controlled by Civil Defence wireless vans.

From 1968, the police took control, with the lead car setting the pace

As Rodney Flowers is precariously held by his trousers, you can almost hear him shout, "There you idiot, Braybrooks, there!" as he tries to explain exactly where Doug Braybrooks should stick the metal flower in his hand. This was in 1978, when all the floats had to be finished as they left the Bulb Auction.

and officers walking round with the floats, particularly the ones with poor visibility, and helping them to negotiate tight corners.

Chief superintendent George Bulman was involved with the parade for many years, and regularly inspected floats to make sure that the drivers had sufficient visibility.

Regular officers and special constables - 150 of them – came from Lincoln, Grantham, Skegness and Boston and the operation was run from the Control Room at the Cattle Market Offices for many years by Inspector Keith Woods.

Many officers would spend so long giving directions, joking with the crowd and preventing people encroaching onto the road, that they ended the day hoarse and footsore. Children would also become separated from their parents in the large crowd and they had to be reunited with their parents.

The traffic had to be controlled and directed to the different car and coach parks. Roads were closed and reopened in a predetermined sequence to allow the parade to pass freely and then to empty the town as quickly as possible afterwards. Emergency vehicles had to be able to pass freely.

Horace Braybrooks and Len van Geest, enjoying the prospect of the first Flower Parade, from their seats on the Tulip Queen's float.

Adam's float crosses High Bridge in 1965. Note Berrills Department Store in the background, with The Ramskin Pub beside it and the rear of the Corn Exchange behind that. Pictured below is the same view in 1982, after Berrills and The Ramskin had gone and the Corn Exchange had been replaced by the Civic Centre.

Spalding Young Farmers, Pete Woodhead, Nick Grundy, Nick Pell and Sarah Tippler,
ready for the 1979 parade.

The large crowds attracted petty criminals and unlicensed street traders.
These were often dealt with by plain clothes officers. Probably the biggest
problems for the police on parade day were drink related. A few people took
too much of an advantage of extended afternoon drinking licences and there
was occasional trouble outside one or two pubs.

One year the police decided to have the pubs close during the parade.
The problem was that when the pubs closed, a lot of toilet facilities were also
lost. The exercise was not repeated.

In 1984 George Bulman retired and the police purse strings began to
tighten and in 1988 three members of the committee, Adrian Chappell,
Adrian van Egmond and Adrian Jansen acted as marshals.

The only committee members to go round with a parade previously were
Brian Drury, when he jumped on a float to move it up after the driver failed

to appear, and ended up driving it all the way round, and Doug Braybrooks as an observer in the police car, (the shouts of "Got you at last Braybrooks" were quite unnecessary).

By 1998 the police required 65 paid stewards, to be provided by the organisers, to match their 65 officers.

The Weather

Any event that is held in the open air in the English spring is bound to be affected by the weather. When the principal component is a spring flower, the chances of disruption are compounded.

Some early parades were postponed by a week, or even more, because of the weather but with the increasingly efficient use of cold stores and more advanced bookings, this practice eventually ceased.

Even so, early or late springs still affected the availability of tulip heads. Sometimes the effect was little more than reducing the choice of colours. On other occasions daffodils and coloured paper had to be used.

One year blue hyacinths, brought over from Holland, along with local daffodils, combined beautifully to provide the perfect colours for British Rail's new high speed 125 train. The scent from the display was exquisite too.

The weather on the day could make conditions unpleasant. Too hot and marching bands suffered and people fainted in the crowd. Too cold and riders on floats would suffer. Heavy rain not only soaked everybody taking part in the parade and turned the field into a quagmire but also reduced attendances and had a drastic effect on takings.

Probably the biggest impact of heavy rain came in 1978, when a torrential downpour on the Friday resulted in the Sir Halley Stewart Field being flooded.

An emergency meeting was held in No. 4 shed and it was agreed that if any floats were to go onto the field on Saturday morning, they would not get off again.

This meant all the attachments that normally took all Saturday morning to put on would have to go on as the floats left the shed at the start of the parade - including the girls.

Brian Drury provided another forklift and with Rodney Flowers on one side and Doug Braybrooks on the other three hours' work were crammed into one.

Media and Celebrities

Over the years, press and television coverage, and even participation has been encouraged by the organisers, to further the publicity of the local bulb industry.

Bill Hunt, the Anglia Television weatherman, was invited to the official reception and would mention Spalding Flower Parade on the Friday evening forecast. Yorkshire Television was a big supporter of the parade, having a stand on the field and supplying celebrities, usually from the cast of Emmerdale, to ride in the parade and sign autographs afterwards.

Blue Peter covered the event, with John Noakes in attendance. The ITV equivalent, Magpie, even entered its own float, with the lovely Jenny Hanley making an appearance.

The parade appeared regularly on local news bulletins and in 1979, Yorkshire Television made a documentary entitled Not A Hundred Miles From Wembley, referring to the fact that there would be more people on the streets of Spalding watching the parade than at Wembley watching the Cup Final on the same afternoon.

Views of tulip fields near Spalding.

Doug Braybrooks and Bertie Wray waiting for the parade to return to the Sir Halley Stewart Field

Doug Braybrooks with one of the John Player girls.

Members of the cast of "Emmerdale Farm" pose with their prized cauliflowers.

The film followed the whole year, from the dismantling of one parade through the planning and creation of the next.

The Villages

Apart from supplying refreshments to visitors on the Tulip Route and decorating their churches, some villages got even more involved in Spalding's parade.

Pinchbeck once entered a float and Long Sutton was in twice. Pinchbeck West had a float for more than 20 years, pulled by two of Sneath's magnificent Percheron heavy horses.

Not only did Moulton Chapel enter a float in Spalding Flower Parade but the village has its own parade the following day.

The Springfields Years

In the mid 1960s South Holland Horticultural Society formed a company called Publicity for British Bulbs and established a show garden at Spalding.

The purpose of the garden was to provide publicity for British bulbs, to educate growers and the public in varieties and the use of bulbs, to form a marketing base for the industry and to provide an amenity for the area.

The project was mostly funded by the industry, with companies and individuals lending or donating anything from £5 to £2,000, one of the largest donors being coal merchants Parson and Snape.

The flower parade also made a large donation, which was reciprocated in years to come. There was also a bank that "listened", under the local management of Les Morton.

The first directors, nominated by South Holland Horticultural Association, were virtually the same as the first Flower Parade Committee, namely; Len van Geest (chairman), Horace Braybrooks (vice-chairman), Ted Grant, Francis Hanson, Do Konynenburg, Percy Taylor and Willis White.

The gardens were called Springfields Gardens and the organising committee was called Springfields Council.

Crowds line the streets of Spalding town centre to welcome the 2004 parade led by Flower Queen Vickie Chapman.

Television Memories was the theme of the 2004 spectacular and what a day it was.
All those involved said they took home some special memories of their own following another great parade.

Clowning around: some of the many charity fundraisers who have taken part in the parade over the years collecting cash for the area's worthy causes.

A Day to Remember was the theme of the 2006 parade. This colourful character salutes VE Day as portrayed by one of the floats from that year.

With the flower parade growing rapidly, it made sense to use their own staff to run it, rather than staff employed by the National Farmers' Union (NFU) so Springfields staff took over the administration of the parade, although NFU personnel continued to be involved voluntarily.

By the late 1970s 20 years of sustained success started to dip and the acreage of tulips grown began to decrease rapidly.

This was mainly due to the increased cost of labour and because the Dutch grew their tulips on much lighter land than ours so they were able to mechanise their bulb lifting and cleaning without damaging the delicate tulip bulb. That meant they could bring their flowers and bulbs into this country at a price with which the British grower could not compete.

Fewer growers could afford to pay for staff to dress floats free of charge and the parade organisers had to pay for more gang labour.

In 1978 it was noted that Geest's bulb acreage was down and the outlook for heads was "grim." It was also pointed out that labour costs for heading had doubled. Other costs crept up as well.

For example, in 1978 there were bills of £100 for refuse collection and £100 for damage to turf on the Sir Halley Stewart Field.

In 1981 the electricity bill for the field was £1,000. Whereas organisers had previously been able to find sheds in which to build the floats free of charge, by 1990 they were having to pay £4,000.

At the same time as labour costs were going up, attendance figures in the Sir Halley Stewart Field, the main source of income, were going down. In 1971 attendance on the Sir Halley Stewart Field over the weekend was 110,000 but by 1977 that figure had dropped to 51,000.

This was reflected in the balance sheet. The first losses started to appear in the mid 1980s. In 1988 the parade lost £12,000 and in 2000 £23,000.

Spalding Flower Parade has always been an event for all the family and 1961 was no exception. Here some youngsters patiently sit on the kerb, eagerly awaiting a glimpse of the first float.

Springfields was now subsidising the parade and digging deep into its reserves to do so. Every attempt was made to cut costs and £1,700 was saved by changing from straw cladding to polythene foam sheeting.

In 1988, South Holland District Council agreed to waive the £600 charge for use of the Sir Halley Stewart Field, to pay half of the St. John Ambulance charge and to provide extra barriers at no cost.

A 1961 view from Chatterton Water Tower showing coaches parked in Winfrey Avenue car park.

Until then, the Flower Parade Committee had had to provide all of the crowd control barriers around town. Councillor Tom Barker joined the committee in March 1989.

In 1988, the Olau Shipping Line offered to sponsor the parade for £45,000 over three years, which was only a temporary relief.

The future of the parade was now seriously in doubt and it was agreed that support was needed from the townspeople who benefited and South Holland District Council.

After the 1995 loss of £27,000 Springfields decided that it could not fund another parade and added that "Spalding needed the parade, the industry did not."

The council had decided to underwrite the parade for up to £15,000. Four more councillors joined the Flower Parade Committee.

Costs continued to increase with the police steadily reducing numbers but requiring the parade organisers to increase their numbers of stewards and marshals.

In 1994 it was decided to introduce street collections for the first time in conjunction with the Rotary organisation. This move was not popular with

This shot of the Winfrey Avenue bus station was captured from way up high in the nearby Chatterton Water Tower and shows John Cresswell's café and the Bulb Auction Halls where construction of the floats took place.

Workers use makeshift platforms to dress a float in the Bulb Auction sheds.

everybody and some float sponsors even threatened to withdraw because they felt that it lowered the tone of the parade.

In 1973 the police had first discussed moving the parade to Springfields and by 1995 the move had become inevitable. When the Cattle Market and the Bulb Auction were closed and work began on the development of it and the Station Yard, into Holland Market, parking for more than 100 coaches was lost.

There was now virtually no parking near the Sir Halley Stewart Field but ample parking at Springfields.

Although the council had removed its charges it was still thought that a

And voilà: one team of float decorators checks the original plans against the finished article.

"Around the world" was the theme of this float which was greeted by hundreds of well-wishers as it wound its way through New Road.

Decorated vehicles also took part in the parade. Margaret's Hairdressers adorned its vehicle with a giant pair of tulip-covered scissors when it took pride of place in the parade.

A Penny Farthing rider, probably from Long Sutton and District Veteran Cycle Club, leads a group of cyclists on bikes from bygone ages through Spalding's Hall Place.

saving of £10,000 could be made, by moving the static display of floats to Springfields.

This saving was made by not having to double up on costs that could be shared with activities on the arena at Springfields, where Brian Willoughby organised a Country Fair.

Over the years, different steps have been taken to involve more people in the organising and support of the flower parade. In 1971 an advisory panel

Spalding Flower Parade has always been an event for all the family - these youngsters took part in the 2004

Thousands of people line the parade route to watch the start of another colourful parade as it winds its way from Springfields into the town centre.

Pupils from the George Farmer Technology College, at Holbeach, were among the hundreds of school children who

was set up, with the intention of involving younger growers. The panel quickly determined that it was important to "impress upon the town that this was their parade, and not just the growers."

By 1992, it appeared that support for the parade, by both locals and South Holland District Council, had declined so much that the council decided not to hang bunting in the town centre and to scale down other events surrounding the parade.

This was the catalyst that brought about a public meeting in the Civic Centre. The meeting was chaired by Len van Geest (Jnr), and present were

This aerial picture shows hundreds of people crammed into Spalding's Market Place to catch a glimpse of the 1963 parade.

representatives of the Flower Parade Committee, South Holland District Council, business groups and interested members of the public.

A committee was formed which introduced South Holland Spring Festival. The president was Len van Geest and it was enthusiastically chaired by Anthony Howling.

On the committee were representatives of the Flower Parade Committee, South Holland District Council, Spalding Chamber of Commerce, the *Lincolnshire Free Press* and *Spalding Guardian* and interested members of the public.

The non-profit making association was formed to co-ordinate and encourage public involvement in an annual Spring Festival, with Spalding Flower Parade as its centre-piece.

Pupils from Spalding's Gleed Schools get in on the act and help prepare for the 1963 event.

This 1963 aerial shot shows the Halley Stewart Field, Chatterton Water Tower, Bulb Auction and Cattle Market with the railway station in the background.

This was to be achieved by working closely with the parade committee, offering support and co-operation to help secure the flower parade's long term future. The committee was responsible for encouraging, co-ordinating and publicising events to be organised by churches, businesses, schools and young people's organisations and giving special attention to children and young people, the disabled and elderly, seeking to involve them wherever possible in the flower parade and festival's activities.

In 1999 George Slinger retired as chairman of the Flower Parade Committee and Peter Atkinson MBE retired as general manager of Springfields.

David Norton became chief executive of Springfields and chairman of the Flower Parade Committee.

In 2003 an arrangement was made with development company Thornfield Properties to develop an eight acre site at Springfields as a shopping outlet. In return Thornfield would invest in the rest of the garden and provide continued support for it and the parade.

South Holland Horticultural Association (NFU) is still involved as custodian of Springfields Horticultural Society, with Lord Taylor of Holbeach as chairman of the society, which maintains the gardens.

In 2005 Spalding Flower Parade and Carnival Trust was formed and is now responsible for staging the parade.

While the trust, chaired by Barry Drew, still aims to promote the horticultural industry, the arts, the environment and social enterprise are now an important part of its brief.

The enormous tulip industry that used to pay for the parade is no more. The parade is now supported by South Holland District Council, Leader Plus, the Arts Council and U.B.S. (after Thornfield), with sponsorship still coming from local businesses, clubs and groups.

There are still several growers among the organisers, but also councillors, teachers and other members of the community. The parade that needed to "project an image of a solid industry," is now very much a town carnival.

It has evolved into a different event from the one first envisaged by a handful of growers in a committee room in Broad Street half a century ago.

What used to be the Flower Parade Committee is now the Operations Committee, or Ops Team, under the direction of long time flower parade vice-chairman Adrian Jansen.

Two important players in Adrian's team are Johnny Walkers and Robin Chappell.

Robin supplied almost all of the tulips for the parade for many years,

Crowds gather outside Spalding's Bull Inn, in Church Gate, in anticipation of the 1966
Spalding Tulip Parade.

and even though he no longer grows tulips, he is still very much involved.
There is also a happy band of volunteers who turn up year in and year out,
to drive floats, marshal and generally help.

The person now behind the designing and building of the floats is Jacquie
Barnes, with the help of welders Richard Creasey and Ian Caudwell. Float
building now takes place at Holbeach Council Depot and dressing is done at
Flint's Farm, Bowmans at Fulney and Robin Chappell's farm.

The tulip heads are now mostly supplied by Moulton Chapel grower Vic Smith, virtually the last commercial tulip grower left in the area.

The floats are slightly smaller than they used to be because of health and safety considerations.

Considering the fact that the industry that started Spalding Flower Parade barely exists anymore and taking into account the health and safety requirements, (the risk assessment document runs to 150 pages), the local growers and people of Spalding can be proud that they have been able to keep it going for so long.

When people hear the name Spalding, they no longer say: "Is that where they make the tennis balls?" but: "That's where they have the flower parade."

The legacy of those tulip pioneers still remains. The fertile soil still produces a multitude of crops, including daffodils.

The distribution service that grew up around the flower industry now distributes for the supermarkets. The flower and food packing industry is thriving.

The business that was started by two Dutch brothers selling tulip bulbs and then became famous for its shipping lines and bananas is now one of the country's biggest fresh and prepared food suppliers, now named the Bakkavor Group.

And Spalding will always be remembered for "Possibly the Greatest Free Show on Earth".

It's party time: a carnival touch has been added to the traditional parade with exotic and flamboyant

A touch of the Notting Hill Carnival has come to the parade in the last few years with brightly coloured costumes,

Bibliography

Spalding and District Bulb Growers and Market Gardeners' Association minutes.
South Holland Horticultural Association minutes.
Spalding Flower Parade Committee minutes.
Spalding Flower Parade programmes.
A History of The Fens of South Lincolnshire – W H Wheeler.
From Punt to Plough - Rex Sly.
The Tulip – Anna Pavord.
Bulbs in Britain, A Century of Growing – Reg Dobbs, OBE.
The Story of The Tulip – Spalding and District Young Farmers' Club.
Spalding Guardian and *Lincolnshire Free Press*.

The End.